THE ROLE OF THE UNITED NATIONS IN INTERNATIONAL PEACEKEEPING

Solomon Hailu

Contents

2

Chapter One: The Indivisibility of Peace

The idea that peace is indivisible has been influential in the theory and practice of security policies for hundreds of years. This has meant several things. The first is that peace and security are intimately linked. When states feel insecure, the individual steps they take to compensate for their perceived vulnerability compromise the security of others and undermine the overall stability of the international system. The second is that the security of all states is undermined if aggression against any of their number is unchecked. The third is that no one state or group of states can combine the incentive, the capacity, and the moral authority to address the problems arising from the first two points. At its simplest, these three things combine to foster the belief in the theory and practice of international relations, that security is a community concern. Following this, states, whatever their individual security concerns or interests, have to address them in a multilateral context. They have an overriding interest in making contributions and sacrifices to express security as a community concern. That is, national security must be addressed through international security.

This key idea had become virtually a consensus position in the discourse of security by the second half of the twentieth century. It is true that states differed on how they interpreted the relationship between national and international security, but, by the end of the Second World War, none could ignore it. Despite this, the idea of the indivisibility of peace has been cast in many forms and institutional expressions. Global and regional institutions have had military and non-military focuses. At this point, it would be valuable to summarize some of the most important approaches to the expressing and addressing the concerns, which are derived from the conviction of the indivisibility of peace and will be discussed in this work. That is because it has been interpreted in changing international (and now global) contexts as well as in the light of changing ideas about the nature of international relations. The idea of the indivisibility of peace has also been influenced by ideologies, conceptions of national interest, and fluctuating views on the possibilities of international society.

Preventive Diplomacy: This is action to prevent disputes from arising between parties, to prevent existing disputes from escalating into conflicts and to limit the spread of conflicts when they occur.[1] In other words, it means diplomatic involvement which occurs before conflicting parties come to blows and seeks to avoid military conflict.[2]

Peace-making: This institutional response to conflict involves diplomatic efforts to end ongoing conflict. As Boutros Ghali put it, "It is an action to bring hostile parties to agreements, essentially through peaceful means such as those foreseen in Charter VI."[3] These activities, which occur while fighting is going on, include the ability to investigate and to

---

[1] Boutros-Gali. (1992). "An Agenda for Peace" United Nations, New York, pp. 11-19.
[2] Snow, D. M. (1993). "Peacekeeping, Peacemaking and Peace-enforcement: the U.S Role in the New International Order." http://carlisle-www.army.mil/usassi/.

[3] Boutros-Gali. "An Agenda for Peace," pp. 11-19.

make suggestions, mediation, reconciliation, and arbitration.[4]

Peacekeeping: This involves a direct deployment of a United Nations presence in the field. Hitherto, practice has been to have the consent of all the parties concerned; although as later discussion will make clear, present and future practice is likely to diverge from this. Deployments involve United Nations military and/or police personnel and frequently (indeed increasingly) civilians as well. Peacekeeping is a technique that expands the possibilities for the prevention of conflict as well as the making of peace.[5] This means that the peacekeepers are invited after a cease-fire has been signed. The peacekeepers are armed with light weapons only. Their task is to physically separate the conflicting parties and monitor their adherence to the cease-fire while negotiations for peace take place.[6] The practice of

---

[4] Snow. "Peacekeeping, Peacemaking and Peace-enforcement."
[5] Boutros-Gali. "An Agenda for Peace," pp. 11-19.
[6] Urquhart, B. (1990). "Beyond the Sheriff's Posse" *Survival* Vol. 32 (3), p. 198.

peacekeeping has been expanded to use increasing force to maintain the peacekeepers' position in the event of the conflicting parties resorting to forceful means again.

Peace Enforcement: Traditionally, the concept refers to collective security schemes that rely on the identification of a guilty party—an aggressor—in any international conflict that involves the (actual or threatened) use of force. Collective security requires action to be taken in order to deter or punish this aggressor. In UN practice, this has involved UN-led multinational military efforts to impose peace against such aggressor states under the authorization of Chapter Vll of the United Nations. The Korean War (1950-1953) and the Gulf War (1990-1991) are the principal examples of this expression of the indivisibility of peace. In both cases, the mandate of the intervention was to restore the sovereignty of the victims of aggression, respectively Kuwait and South Korea. However, in the context of the 1990s, peace-enforcement is likely to involve the violation of state sovereignty, particularly if the mission takes place on the soil of the combatant who opposes peace and does not invite the peace enforcers. The United Nations Operation in Somalia (UNOSOM) 1992-1995 and United Nations Assistance for Rwanda (UNAMIR) 1994 are cases in point where the classic understanding of aggression has been adapted and expanded.[7] In these cases, a new concept and practice of intervention called, "forceful humanitarian intervention" has been developed. This takes as its main purpose protecting civilian victims of the ongoing armed conflict by creating a safety zone to against human rights abuse. For example, during the Gulf war, the Kurds were protected by the allied forces from attacks by Iraqi forces. The mission also involved providing them with humanitarian assistance (food and medicine). The mission used military means to sustain relief efforts, as did the one in Somalia. The Security Council authorised peace enforcement based on article Vll of the UN Charter on the grounds that "the magnitude of the human

---

[7] Snow. "Peacekeeping, Peacemaking and Peace-enforcement."

tragedy constitutes a threat to international peace and security"[8]. Arguably, this constitutes a sweeping adaptation of the original concept of "security," which underpinned Chapter VII, the source of legitimacy for the operation itself.

Peace Building: This too is a contemporary adaptation and extension of multilateral concerns and the indivisibility of peace. It involves action to identify and support structures that will tend to strengthen and solidify peace, in order to avoid a relapse into conflict. In attempting to consolidate peace, peace building involves among other things: [9]

- Military and security activities such as disarmament, demobilization of combatants, and destruction of arms as well as re-integration of forces and de mining.
- Humanitarian activities, including repatriation and resettlement of refugees, along with infrastructural activities such as:

---

[8] Watson, R. and others. "It Is Our Fight"
Newsweek, December 14, 1992, p. 35.
[9] Boutros-Gali. "An Agenda for Peace," pp. 11-19.

building houses and health and education institutions.

- Political action such as fostering good-governance, institutional reforms, election monitoring, the promotion of respect for human rights, the reform of judiciary and police, and the investigation of crime.

- Economic and Social activities involving the reconstruction of war-torn economies, major infrastructural development, which may be carried out by UN organs such as the UNDP and financed by international financial institutions such as the World Bank, the IMF, and international donor communities.

This summary gives an idea of the range of contemporary instruments and resources that express the international dimension of security policies. This, in turn, helps to illustrate the adaptive and developmental dimensions of the belief in the idea of the indivisibility of peace.

In so far as there has been a consensus on the indivisibility of peace, it originated in a general

11

agreement that some sort of international body has to be established to mobilise and pool the resources of sovereign states to administer and lead a multinational force against aggressors.

This idea was put into effect by the creation of the League of Nations in 1919 and the United Nations in 1945. The League of Nations was created as the first comprehensive international collective security institution, in the hope of averting global war after the disaster of WWI. The logic behind the formation of the League of Nations was to enforce collective security action to maintain international peace and order. However, the League could not perform its duties as set out in its covenant. The most important reason was lack of genuine commitment on the side of its members to turn the text of the covenant into action against the lawbreaker.

The United Nations sought to learn from the League's experience in trying to deal with the matter of maintaining international peace and security. It soon became clear however that the UN faced different conditions. These were responsible for doctrinal shifts in the UN and dilution of members' commitment to the success of its objectives. In its almost six decades of existence, the UN has recorded both successes and failures. To illustrate this, this study divides UN peacekeeping operations into two general categories. The first is traditional or classical peacekeeping, which evolved during the Cold War (1948-1989), principally as a substitute for the collective security provisions of the Charter, which were rendered inoperable by the clash of superpower interests and the resulting institutional stalemate. In this context, the UN in most cases involved itself in inter-state conflicts. In cases of this sort, the UN widely implemented three principles of peacekeeping doctrine. These were consent, impartiality, and non-or minimum use of force. This study argues that during its Cold War interventions, these three main principles of intervention helped the UN to play a constructive role and, from time to time, achieve significant successes.

The UN's post-Cold War intervention is labelled "modern peacekeeping." In this context, the nature of intervention has changed along with dramatic changes in the nature of conflicts. Most of the conflicts during this period have been intra-state. This has made it difficult for the UN to mount peacekeeping operations using its restricted principles of Cold War intervention. Applying consent, impartiality and minimum use of force as preconditions for intervention became difficult in a new situation, no matter how well they had served during the Cold War. Intervention can now be mounted without the consent of the warring parties, involving greater force than used to be the case. The post-Cold War conflicts brought the so-called "failed" or "collapsed" states to prominence in the international system. The UN had little experience in dealing with such deadly civil wars that caused total state emergencies. The UN's sole experience in dealing with deadly civil wars and collapsed states was in the isolated case of the Congo as far back as the early 1960s, in the different context of the Cold War. In dealing with these new developments, the UN has suffered from doctrinal restrictions. For example, Article 2 (7) of its Charter states that the UN should not intervene in matters essentially within the domestic jurisdiction of any state. Despite this limitation, UN forces have intervened in zones of conflict without invitation to save the civilian victims. The UN intervention in Somalia (1993-94) is a case in point. In response to new kinds of conflict, the UN has also added new ingredients to its post-Cold War peacekeeping profile. Among these are what this study calls "forceful humanitarian intervention" and "post-conflict state reconstruction."

Chapter Two: The Origin of the Idea of Collective Security

The assumption that international peace and security can be achieved only through collective measures was initially proposed in the beginning of the 18th century by Immanuel Kant. According to Kant, no universal Leviathan was necessary; instead, a large federation of committed states could promote and maintain international peace. He criticised the idea that peace can be preserved under a mere balance-of-power system based on the idea that each state was invested with an equal right to resort to war. Equally, he rejected the view that any idea of an international organization for maintaining peace should be regarded as utopian and unable to contain devastating war among European Christian states.[10]

The distinctions between the schools of balance of power and collective security as approaches to

---

[10] Negretto, G. T. (1993). "Kant and the Illusion of Collective Security." *Journal of International Affairs* Vol. 46 (2), p. 501.

international security are confused by the various usages of the concept "balance of power" in the theory and practice of international relations. The label has been attached to a wide range of practices, values, and prescriptions to do with maintaining order among sovereign states. However, two things in particular stand out as common features in these various usages.

The first is that the balance of power—however understood—has as its principal objective the preservation of the system of sovereign states that enshrines the independence of all its members. It is not, then, a system (or a policy, or a prescription, or a universal law of state behaviour) whose overriding goal is the preservation of peace. Indeed, it may well be a prescription for war against a rising power that threatens the overall system. In theory at least, the balance of power does not require all acts of interstate violence to be deterred or punished, only those that threaten the overall integrity of the system. Indeed, since the balance of power is underpinned by realist assumptions about the legitimacy of the self-interested pursuit of power in the interests of security and self-realization of states, violence that does not threaten the system is tolerated, and violence that preserves it is celebrated.

It follows from these realist assumptions and from the centrality of sovereign independence, that the balance of power is a prescription for self-help that does not require an overarching authority.

In theory, the balance-of-power system requires only armies and diplomacy as the "perennial instruments of foreign policy." However, for these instruments to be effective, there are additional requirements, including reliable information about other states intentions and capabilities as well as the ability to interpret it without distortion. At bottom, the balance of power works best where states have a common understanding of the system in which they co-exist and a shared belief that it is in their common interests to sustain it. This in turn requires an absence of sharp ideological division and that no powerful state or group of states should feel excluded or alienated.

It is for this reason that the so-called Concert of Europe is often held up as the most successful example of order keeping through the balance of power. In reality, the Concert was a variety of semi-formal diplomatic understandings that helped govern the international relations of the European great powers between 1815 and the outbreak of the First World War in 1914. The degree of formality and the scope of the understandings varied, ultimately breaking down as tensions surrounding the creation of a powerful new German state in 1870 made themselves felt in the last quarter of the 19th century and the first decade of the 20th. However, several principles were consistent. Principal among them was the imperative that self-interest could only be advanced within a general context of system preservation. Another imperative was that all great powers had a legitimate interest in all the major issues (including especially the so-called Eastern Question), and all had to be consulted and, if necessary, compensated when one of their number made gains.

The example of the Concert of Europe seems to suggest that that as the number of states increases and as technology makes them increasingly interdependent, yet increasingly capable of destroying each other, the conditions for the success of balance of power as a model of order keeping multiply. The need for developed structures or agencies becomes apparent and the logic of community force, rather than unregulated self-help, seems attractive as the guarantor of security.

Arguably, it is in the absence of these latter two qualities that the inadequacies of the balance of power are most clearly seen, leading to the conclusion that a more formal organization of mutual agreement and power to keep the peace is required.

In contrast to the balance of power, collective security must be created through an international organization capable of organizing co-operation among states for the maintenance of peace.[11] However, Kant asserted that such a league should not

---

[11] Negretto. "Kant and the Illusion of Collective Security," p. 501.

be a world governing body. Rather, it should be an executive body entitled to enforce peace by means of collective coercion against aggressor states. It does not tend to any domination over the power of the state itself and does not require that members need to submit to civil laws and their compulsion, as "men in the state of nature must submit."[12] The federation would become so strong as to enforce peace against aggressor states.[13] In other words, a coalition force is necessary to serve as a real deterrent to any aggressor.[14] As Woodrow Wilson argued:

> "... it will be absolutely necessary that force be created ... so much greater than the force of any nation now engaged or any alliance hitherto forced or projected that no nation, no

---

[12] *Kant on History* Beck, W. L. (ed.) and translator (1967) New York, Boobs-Merrill, p. 100.
[13] Negretto, "Kant and the Illusion of Collective Security," p. 501.
[14] Negretto, "Kant and the Illusion of Collective Security," p. 501.

probable combination of nations could face or withstand."[15]

While Wilson emphasises sheer military power in this conception of deterrence, arguably another key component is the moral weight of community consensus, which would wield this military power. Seen in this light, collective security depends on some form of international body which needs to be established to mobilize and pool the support and resources of sovereign states, as well as to administer and lead a multinational force to enforce peace.

It often argued that there is a profound similarity between Kant's ideas and the international collective security systems and the institutions created in the twentieth century, the League of Nations and the United Nations. [16] Both of these institutions came into existence based on the assumption that some

---

[15] Wilson, W. (1996). "A League of Peace" David, L. L. (ed.). *The Puritan Ethic in United States Foreign Policy Princeton*, NJ: Van Nostrand, p. 183.

[16] Negretto. "Kant and the Illusion of Collective Security," p. 501.

kind of international organization must be created if war is to be avoided or at least limited. In the first place, the study will discuss the League of Nations collective security system and thereafter, its "heir," the UN.

Chapter Three: The Birth of the League of Nations

The first attempt to establish collective security as a new model was made after the First World War, and it was embodied in the creation of the League of Nations. It has been argued that the "new utopia was the desire of western statesman toward the end of the First World War to revive ideas about international peace offered by the earlier philosophers."[17] Whatever the influence of the ideas of these philosophers, the experience of the First World War seemed to make it plain that questions of war and peace could no longer be dealt with as questions of national security alone, but that national security could only be sought within a context of international security, in which all states had a common interest in peace. It was not merely that technology had endowed states with means to destroy on an industrial scale, which they could not themselves

---

[17] Negretto. "Kant and the Illusion of Collective Security," p. 501.

control. It was also that the destructiveness of modern war obviously made itself felt in the destruction of whole social and political orders.

These lessons would have been profound enough on their own, but they were given further point by the changing distribution of power in international relations. The growing power and influence of the USA in international relations was sufficiently apparent to European leaders for US President Woodrow Wilson's views on the bankruptcy of the "old diplomacy" of alliances and secret treaties to be decisive. These views led Wilson to echo the proponents of the idea of collective security in previous centuries when he said that:

> "some method of international co-operation was needed to maintain international peace and prevent future wars. …mere agreements, …may not make peace secure…"[18]

---

[18] Wilson. "A League of Peace," p. 183.

He went on to say that the new model for peace must be "not a balance-of-power, but a community of power; not organised rivalries, but an organised common peace."[19] To achieve this common goal, an international executive body was wanted to mobilise and co-ordinate the support of the states. It would command and direct an unbeatable international coalition force and deter the aggressor in the name of the international community. The belief that peace is indivisible underpinned this collective answer to the problems of insecurity. Under Article 11 of the Covenant of the League of Nations, any war or threat of war, whether immediately affecting any of the members of the League or not, was declared a matter of concern to the whole League. The Covenant stipulated pacific resolution of disputes (Articles 12, 13 and 15) and forceful resort (first economic sanctions followed by military actions) against the aggressor. Article 16 of the Covenant states that if any League member or non-member state were to resort war in violation of the peaceful settlements of

---

[19] Wilson. "A League of Peace," p. 183.

disputes, this should be regarded ipso facto as an act of war against all members of the League. Despite the goals prescribed in its Covenant, the League of Nations did not succeed in maintaining international peace and order.

Before assessing the failure of the League and the influence this had on later attempts at institutional order keeping in international relations, it is important to try to be clear about the nature of the organization. In some senses, the League—as noted above—did indeed represent a rejection of the past. However, in other respects, it built heavily on the conventions and practices of traditional international relations, and this prevented it from being a wholly radical departure into an alternative new world. After all, whatever the disillusion over the cost of the balance of power in lives and destruction, in fact, the system had worked. The aggressor had been punished and was now prostrate. The rights of small nations—Belgium and Serbia—had been upheld. Britain at the beginning and America at the end of the war had acted as the balancers in classic fashion.

It was the price, not the principle that was the problem. The solution was to make security a community concern and bind all to a conception of a formalized balance of power in which force would never have to be used and the price would never again have to be paid.

Rather than an eruption of idealism, the League represented, in the eyes at least of the European great powers Britain and France, the opportunity to add a community dimension to their efforts to achieve security. Exhaustion and over-commitment prevented them from achieving it by traditional foreign policy alone, so the burden would be shared—or preferably shifted.

In these senses, the League was not so much a fresh start as it was a compromise with the past. Moreover, it had continually to adjust and compromise to the present in the shape—for instance, of the relapse of America into isolation and the rise of aggressive, revisionist regimes, first in Italy, then in Germany and finally, Japan. These ambiguities did not necessarily doom the League to failure, but they provided a context in which the maintenance of international peace and security became intolerably difficult.

The major reasons for the failure of the League of Nations are conventionally summarized in the following terms: the reluctance of member states to take coercive action against the lawbreaker; the issue of national interest and lack of commitment to international law; the power of aggressors to defy deterrence; changes in the League's constitution. The League's members simply pledged to confront aggression, rather than obligate themselves, to confront it.[20] In practice, they had grave reservations about the desirability of military action against aggression which hampered the League in taking enforcement action.[21] Essentially, the problem was

---

[20] Albright, M. K. (1993). "Building a Collective Security System." *US Department of State Dispatch* Vol. 4 (19), pp. 334.

[21] Claude, Inis L. Jr. (1956). *Swords into Plowshares: the Problems and Progress of International Organization*. New York, Random House, p. 153.

that states hoped that the League would solve their problems merely by coming into existence. The belief in the deterrent effect of (the threat of) community action would be a substitute for the use of force, rather than a commitment to it. Secondly, in the clash of self-and collective interests, members opted for the former. As a case in point, Britain and France, the two big powers on which the League depended, refused to send troops in response to the Japanese invasion of the Chinese territory, Manchuria, in 1931. They feared a possible Japanese attack on their colonial territories in the Far East. In any case, the Manchuria issue was clouded by specific aspects of the situation, including Japan's "special treaty rights" in the area, which included the presence of a Japanese army as well as the chaotic condition of China at the time. Complexities of this sort are very useful as obstacles to action for states whose commitment and resources are thin in the first place.

Others like Germany and Italy, the so-called "have-not powers" or "revisionist" powers who were disappointed with the Versailles settlement, were encouraged by the Japanese occupation and saw it as an example to follow. Soon after they withdrew from the League in mid 1930s, Italy invaded Ethiopia. After Italian invasion of Ethiopia in 1935, Emperor Haile Selassie made a speech of warning in his address to the League Assembly, "…Ethiopia may seem far away to Europe, but soon enough they too would be victims of aggression"[22] As with the Manchuria situation, the victim in Ethiopia was not only far from the most vital interests of Britain and France, but also the local balance of power favored the aggressor. However, there was another factor in the case of the luckless Ethiopia.

The essential difficulty was that Britain and France, the two powers on whom the League relied, had dual foreign policies. They hoped to practice power politics as well as collective security. In this form of traditional diplomacy, Italy would be used to

---

[22] Roskin, M. G. and Berry, N. O. (1997). *The New World of International Relations*. New Jersey, Prentice Hall, pp. 349-354.

counterbalance Germany. In the end, they fell between the two policies, failing either to appease Italy, or use the League firmly to deter aggression. The results were disastrous for their foreign policies, the League and the peace of the world.

Thirdly, there was a lack of commitment to international law. As Negretto notes,

> "the main function of international law is to reflect the common values and principles accepted by the international community in a given historical period. ...The proscription of war as a means of international policy, the pacific settlement of disputes, and even the commitment to an international organization for the improvement of the world order, cannot be realized until states and their leaders freely accept the mutual benefits of the maintenance of peace."[23]

---

[23] Negretto. "Kant and the Illusion of Collective Security," p. 534.

Germany's foreign minister, Baron Neurath pronounced an unbeliever's verdict on the dying condition of the League of Nations in 1937. His comment on members' lack of commitment to enforce collective security under the aegis of the League of Nations had some truth in it. He said that "in politics, even in peace politics, success is what counts, not the mere announcements of beautiful aims, which may be enticing, but which are in practice unattainable and therefore worthless."[24] This was particularly evident when the crisis directly involved great powers. As Austen Chamberlain put it in reference to German and Italian aggression, "The League could make a contribution when sparrows were quarreling but was of little avail when eagles were fighting"[25]

---

[24] "Reports and Papers from the Foreign Office Confidential Print Part II Series." *The League of Nations* Maryland: University Publications of America, Vol. 2. (1992), p. 332.
[25] Nish, I. (1993). *Japan's Struggle with Internationalism: Japan, China and the League of Nations, 1931.* London, Kegan Paul International, p. 239.

Fourthly, when the power of the aggressor is too strong to be deterred, collective security is undermined. When the revisionist, aggressor states established their triple alliance this was a formidable grouping outside the League concentration of power. In any case, collective security under the League was not universal since the US was not a member. The absence of the world's greatest economic power— even it was not in the first military rank—was crucial for the Leagues future.

Fifthly, some authorities argue that the League developed constitutional and legal impediments to its own governing text as time went on. In 1921, the Assembly of the League adopted resolutions, declaring that for each state the application of economic sanctions against aggressor states under article 16 was optional, not mandatory.[26]

In defense of the League and collective security, other authorities claim that it is unfair to condemn the

---

[26] Bennet, A. L. (1995). *International Organizations: Principles and Issues*. New Jersey, Prentice Hall, p. 147.

League's efforts because the system was never really tried. Had it not been for the confused purposes of Britain and France and the isolation of the USA, the league would not have been toothless.[27] Effectively, this says that the League did not fail but members failed the League by being sluggish to enforce the covenant. From this standpoint, if none of the members of the League moves, the League itself cannot move.[28] It was for these reasons that the League could not stop the occurrence of WWII.

The failure of the League left lessons that present-day collective security organizations require the political willingness and military preparedness of member states to act effectively to maintain global peace. In the first place, the League experience demonstrated that small, weak states saw collective security arrangements in different ways from large, powerful ones. Where the former saw benefits, the latter saw costs. The former believed that

---

[27] Roskin and Berry. *The New World of International Relations,* p. 354.
[28] Roskin and Berry. *The New World of International Relations*, pp. 379-380.

multilateralism should be an all-embracing system the latter wished to combine it with national security policies. And perhaps above all, the strong were more sensitive than the weak to the (arguably fatal) contradiction that lies at the heart of all multilateral security initiatives; in order to preserve sovereignty through community, states have to give up some degree of sovereign choice to a multilateral body. Although the context has changed again and again since the death of the League in 1940, the lessons have continued to recur.

Chapter Four: The UN Collective Security System: Theory and Practice of Peacekeeping

The United Nations could be described, with considerable justification, as a revised version of the League.

> "Many of its features were indicative of conscious effort to avoid the deficiencies of the previous world organization, - especially in non-political fields, such as economic, social, legal matters and structural arrangements like General Assembly and the Secretariat—but to strengthen the institutional system at points where weakness had become evident, and to project into the progressive future."[29]

By 1945, Western—and particularly American—conceptions of the theory and practice of international relations had become powerfully influenced by "realist'" assumptions. The combined

---

[29] Claude, Inis L. Jr. (1962). *Power and International Relations,* New York, Random House, pp. 60-61.

effect of these was to portray a world in which self-interest expressed in terms of power competition is the predominant motivating force in system of states characterized by decentralized authority and weak community structures. UN institutions in the security field were built on two principles that grew out of this worldview.

The first was that countervailing power organized by an executive committee of the world's strongest states into an overwhelming deterrent would be necessary to deal with the aggressor states, which would be thrown up by the realist conditions of the international system. The second was the principle that such an executive committee would have to include all the world's greatest powers, their status as such would have to be recognized with privileges to go with their responsibilities, and they would be able to act in their executive function only as long as their own vital interests (however they cared to define them) were not at stake.

Out of these assumptions and principles the Security Council, with its veto powers and (never to be realized) plans for permanent military forces at its disposal, was created. In this way, the collective security plans of the UN addressed the security problems of states by aspiring to mobilize and coordinate the capacities of the most powerful states for policing responsibilities and duties in the belief that they would regard the experience of the previous decade as proof positive that the indivisibility of peace was a reality and the key to security for all states.

Nevertheless, although these institutional arrangements represented a conscious effort to replace the "idealism" of the League with a tougher stance on security issues, the UN's structures retained a considerable amount of the League's approach to reducing conflict through the peaceful resolution of disputes, disarmament and preventive diplomacy. As with its predecessor, the assumption behind the UN's two-dimensional approach to security was that the political and diplomatic approach would at best actually ward off armed conflict and at worst, clarify who the aggressor was and prepare the ground for punitive action.[30]

Since 1945, then the UN has been undertaking measures under its various provisions for keeping order. There have been "successes" and "failures" in these activities. The next part of study will focus on the challenges the UN has been facing during the past five decades of service in the changing security environment and the adaptations that its practice has reflected in order to cope with changing threats to security.

The United Nations has been the principal global body dealing with maintaining international peace and security. Its charter states (Article 1:1) that one of the raisons d'être for the birth of the United Nations was

> to maintain international peace and security, and to this end: to take effective collective measures for the prevention and removal of threats to

---

[30] Roskin and Berry. *The New World of International Relations,* p. 354.

the peace, and the suppression of acts of aggression or other breaches of the peace, and to bring about by peaceful means, and in conformity with the principles of justice and international law, adjustment or settlement of international disputes or situations which might lead to breach of the peace.

Within the UN structure, the Security Council has received the mandate of handling international security issues. The United Nations Charter (article 24) granted the Security Council the responsibility for utilizing every possible way to restore or maintain international peace. Among these are:

- Seeking political and diplomatic solutions, involving peaceful resolution of disputes under chapter VI of the UN Charter, including the pacific resolution of disputes, through diplomatic activities like negotiation, mediation, arbitration and conciliation of the disputing parties.

- Forceful means of restoring peace under the authorization of chapter VII of the UN, which allows both military and non-military actions, such as economic sanctions against a law breaker or aggressor in order to restore international peace.

Chapter Five: From Collective Security to Peacekeeping

The post war distribution of power and the UN Charter, which reflected it in so many ways (notably in the composition and powers of the security council), left the UN with collective security provisions that equipped it well to deal with the security problems of the 1930s. Under the UN's classic collective security provisions, a lone revisionist aggressor could be met with the combined weight of the international community—represented by a concert of the greatest powers armed with legitimate military powers—either to persuade, deter or punish it, through a range of diplomatic, sanctioning, or military means.

Two related developments frustrated this vision of order and international security through community action delegated to the most powerful states in the belief that they alone could achieve truly collective security. The first was the end of the wartime alliance on which the hopes of concert lay. Guided by fundamentally opposed views of international order and facing each other over the ruins of Europe, as well as in Asia, where the colonial order had been shattered by first the success and then the defeat of Japanese expansionism, the USA and the USSR could not form the basis of order through a concert of the great powers that the UN charter envisaged.

In the second place, this situation of rival social systems and undeclared hostilities spread by the growth of rival alliance systems not only attacked the practicality of the UN collective security system by undermining the core of community power on which the certainty of punishment for an aggressor should rest. It also undermined the principle of collective security, which required a clear community consensus (a tenuous possibility at best) on the nature of aggression and the identification of the aggressor. This simplistic analysis of what, throughout the twentieth century had become increasingly complex conflicts, became even less likely to achieve. Where some states—notably in the Middle East—existed in a semi-permanent condition of war and where Cold

War allegiances combined with the revolutionary possibilities of decolonization and civil war, intervention, proxy wars, and wars of liberation, aggression resisted consensual definition and identification.

As a result, since the formation of the United Nations in 1945, the UN Security Council has authorised only five military actions based on Chapter VII of its Charter. The only enforcement action that took place during the Cold War was during the Korean War (1950-1954). The others, which were undertaken after the end of the Cold War, were Kuwait (1990), Somalia (1992), Rwanda (1994), and Haiti (1994).

It has been argued that many interstate conflicts during the Cold War period should have attracted the UN's coercive measures. After all, article 2(4) of the Charter effectively outlaws interstate war:

> "All members shall refrain in their international relations from the threat of use of force against the territorial integrity of or political independence

of any state…The only exception to this rule is action in self-defence."[31]

Following this reasoning, Parsons and others argue that during the Cold War many interstate wars have been in clear violation of Article 2(4) of the Charter and that the UN failed to authorise military measure according to Chapter Vll. Examples they cite include the several wars between Israel and the Arab states, the South African incursions into Angola, the Iran Iraq war, the Falklands war, Libya-Chad, China-Vietnam, the Turkish invasion of Cyprus, and the Suez Canal Crisis.[32]

They further argue that almost throughout its Cold War existence, the United Nations has had to act as an instrument of persuasion rather than coercion. All but a handful of the nearly 700 resolutions adopted

---

[31] Bailey, S. D. and Daws, S. (1998). *The Procedures of the Security Council.* Oxford, Clarendon Press, p. 356.
[32] Campbell, K. M. and others. (1990). "Superpowers and UN Peacekeeping." *Harvard International Review.* Vol.12 (2), p. 23.

during the Cold War by the Security Council have been adopted under Chapter VI of the Charter (the pacific settlement of disputes)[33] Under Chapter VI, the parties, not the Security Council, are the prime movers in the search for settlement and the Council has only recommendatory powers. They are there not to enforce peace but to discourage parties from resuming hostilities.[34]

Of the five actions that serve as exceptions to what is often described as the UN's "paralysis" in this field, only two, Korea and the Gulf in 1990/1, rank as true collective security actions. In each case, there are substantial reasons for regarding the circumstances under which they took place as exceptional. Although one of these major cases took place under Cold War conditions and the other at the beginning of the post-Cold War era, they had important things

---

[33] Roskin and Berry. *The New World of International Relations*, p. 354.
[34] Parsons and others. "The United Nations After the Gulf War." http://httpweb12.epnet.com.

in common, which allowed the UN to operate in ways which were usually denied it.

In each case, there was an unusually clear-cut act of cross-border aggression by conventional armed forces. In the second place, circumstances in each case ensured that the aggressor was isolated. In the case of Korea, the absence of the USSR from the major organs of the UN as part of a diplomatic protest allowed the US and its western allies to circumvent what would inevitably have been obstructive action by the USSR, by "creatively" using their majority in the General Assembly, under the "Uniting for Peace Resolution" and authorizing a US-led and dominated force to repel the North Korean invasion of South Korea.

Similarly, when Iraq's forces invaded Kuwait and precipitated the Gulf crisis of 1990/1, the aggression was unusually clear-cut and hard to ignore. This in of itself contributed to the isolation of Iraq's leader, Saddam Hussein, but regional rivalries and fears of augmented Iraqi power helped sway Arab states who might otherwise have balked at the prospect of enforcement action led by the USA against one of their members. Despite the political and military success of the American-led Gulf War coalition, under the auspices of the United Nations collective security provisions, the enforcement action did not lead to an immediate and durable renewal of collective security under the UN as many hoped at the time it would.

- The stunning success of the military action, revealing the sheer disproportionate extent of American power, gave rise to fears of what has come to be known as "unilateralism." This is the perceived tendency for America to rule as a single superpower, ruthlessly using the UN (and other multilateral bodies) as legitimizing instruments of its own power and interests
- As the crisis in the Balkans seemed to demonstrate, internal conflict, rather than easily targeted aggression,

remained the norm and the "Kuwait" paradigm of cross-border invasion was an aberration

- The Balkans also showed—through differences between Europe and America, Russia's desire to protect the interests of the Yugoslav Serbs and in China's fear of untrammelled American power—that the politics of the post-Cold War era could be as obstructive as the East-West conflict and even more complicated

- The military success of the coalition attack on Saddam Hussein's forces was greatly undermined by the political confusion over what to do with the victory. By leaving the Iraqi leader in power, after first encouraging then stepping back from internal revolt against him, the Bush administration's policy revealed the limitations of a collective security system that focused narrowly and exclusively on the military defeat of an aggressor.

It is against the background of the UN's experience of collective security that the development of its capacities for peacekeeping should be considered. To summarize, the UN equipped itself with collective security provisions which did not fit the post-1945 world in which they were supposed to operate. They needed a durable consensus that transcended particular political configurations of each conflict situation in order to make them work as envisaged. Neither in the Cold War, nor even in the post-Cold War world has this been forthcoming. What is more, the kind of aggression which the collective security system of the UN was designed to deter or punish, has rarely been a feature of the conflicts of the past half century.

In this light, it is scarcely surprising that the UN should have broadened and adapted its various mandates for peace and security. A wider range of problems and a more creative—if usually only partial

—range of solutions have been developed, reflecting, among other important features, a broadening range of membership, which brought different perspectives and capabilities as the expansion of the UN took place, principally under the influence of decolonization.

Chapter Six: UN Peacekeeping

During the course of the Cold War (1948-1988), the UN undertook fifteen peacekeeping operations[35] under what, by necessity, were fairly free interpretations of the original collective security concept. It is usual to stress that the UN adapted to situations not envisaged under the charter, in which peacekeepers typically served two functions. These were observing the peace (monitoring and reporting on the maintenance of cease-fires) and actively keeping the peace by providing law and order or separating warring armies by establishing a buffer zone.[36] The UN took on its first peacekeeping mission in 1948 after the end of the first Arab-Israeli war in June 1948. In this case, the UN deployed its observer mission, the UN Truce Supervision

---

[35] Mills, G. and Cilliers, J. (1999). *From Peacekeeping to Complex Emergencies: Peace Support Operations in Africa.* Johannesburg, Institute for Security Studies and South African Institute of International Affairs, p. 1.

[36] Parsons and others. "The United Nations After the Gulf War."

Organization (UNTSO) to monitor cease-fire, truce and armistice agreements in disputed areas. This kind of peacekeeping mission came to be known as "classical" or "traditional" peacekeeping,[37] whereby the UN principles of consent, impartiality and non or minimum use of force were doctrinally implemented as a base for any peacekeeping operation.

Consent means establishing agreement with a disputing party or parties and/or being licensed or given approval to intervene by a party or parties directly involved in the conflict to intervene. The rationale behind consent was that the belligerent parties would commit themselves to co-operate with the third party, the UN, to bring about a lasting solution to an already existing source of friction. This would allow more freedom and legitimacy to the UN in implementing its peacekeeping mandate.

Impartiality means being independent and taking no side. It is a key element in intervention. Tharoor points out that:

---

[37] Mills and Cilliers. *From Peacekeeping to Complex Emergencies,* p.1.

"impartiality is the oxygen of peacekeeping: the only way peacekeepers can work is by being trusted by both sides, being clear and transparent in their dealings, and keeping lines of communication open. The moment they lose this trust, the moment they are seen by one side as the 'enemy', they become part of the problem they were sent to solve."[38]

This means that before landing on the soil of the troubled territory, the third party which is involved as a peacekeeper should have to make clear the basis of its interventionist agenda beforehand. It should persuade all contenders with regard to its impartiality, the duration of the operation and have its identity or the mark of its own peacekeeping force (for instance, operating under the UN flag and with blue helmets to avoid confusion among the warring parties). There is a need also to prove its impartiality to the warring parties in order to maintain trust and confidence in every step taken during the operation.

---

[38] Tharoor, S. (1995-96). "Should UN Peacekeeping go to Basics." *Survival* 37 (4), p. 58.

On the other hand, the warring parties should also prove their acceptance of the third party by signing protocols and committing to terms of agreement, for the peacekeepers to feel legitimized and to move freely to achieve the ultimate goal. For instance, Ethiopia and Eritrea have accepted the United Nations Mission in Ethiopia and Eritrea (UNMEE) to help settle their border conflict.[39] Therefore, to keep the peacekeeping mission alive, a "genuine" position of impartiality on the peacekeeper's side is needed. The commitment of the conflicting parties to agreement concerning the impartiality of the peacekeeping force is also an essential factor.

The impartiality of the UN force may be challenged in situations where a local dispute has cross-border implications, or international dimensions. Belligerents might suspect the involvement of contingents from certain countries in multinational peacekeeping operations to be partial or partisan. For

---

[39] Malan, M. (2000). "UN Peace Operations: A Status Report." Institute for Security Studies, Pretoria, p. 2.

instance, as this study will demonstrate in its six chapter, the United Nations Organization Mission in the Democratic Republic of the Congo (MONIC) does not include military or civilian personnel from the DRC's neighboring countries, especially those that have embroiled themselves by siding with one of the conflicting parties.[40] Therefore, in cases like these, it is mandatory for the UN to consult the conflicting parties before recruiting troops from contributing countries. In most cases during the cold-war interventions, the UN developed a practice of avoiding using troops from the five permanent members of the Security Council (especially China and the two superpowers) and forces from neighboring countries.[41]

The advantages of these practices were obvious; local conflicts were insulated from both Cold War and regional rivalry.[42] The possible disadvantage is that by doing so the forces from the UN sometimes

[40] Malan. "UN Peace Operations," p. 2.
[41] Roberts, A. (1994). "The Crisis in UN Peacekeeping." *Survival* Vol. 35(3), p. 95.
[42] Roberts. "The Crisis in UN Peacekeeping," p. 95.

lacked the authority and strength of the superpowers, or alternatively they lacked the local knowledge, interest and staying power that a neighbouring power might have had.[43]

The UN's principle of non-use of force was first implemented in the UNTSO. In this case, the observer missions were deployed unarmed. The reason behind this was that possible antagonists would be less likely to use their arms against unarmed personnel.[44] Secondly, as the case of UNTSO showed, the UN mission was deployed by consent among the warring parties and was accepted by both parties as a neutral body. Hence, the already established solid agreement between the UN and the belligerents, based on the principles of consent and impartiality, could help to build confidence and trust on the side of the UN missions to participate unarmed. In other words, it also means, as Mark Malan puts it, "that impartiality would bolster the

---

[43] Roberts. "The Crisis in UN Peacekeeping," p. 95.
[44] Malan, M. (1997). "A Concise Conceptual History of UN Peace Operations." *African Security Review* Vol. 6 (1), p. 19.

credibility and legitimacy of the UN force and reduce the likelihood of using force to accomplish mission objectives."[45] This means that the principle of non-use of arms is valid as long as the protagonists are committed to the original terms of agreements throughout the UN presence. Otherwise, in case of change of mind by a party or parties involved in the conflict (for instance, due to sudden escalation of uncertainty that questions the entire presence of the UN force) the threat of collapse and disaster would be very real. For instance, the United Nations Mission in Sierra Leone (UNMSIL) has faced attack from the rebels[46] and the termination of the UN Mission in Angola in February 1999 came after both the government and the rebel movement repeatedly flouted the various peace agreements they signed."[47]

---

[45] Malan. "A Concise History of UN Peace Operations," p. 20.
[46] "Attack on UN Force in Sierra Leone Has Broader Impact." (2005). *AP Worldstream.*
[47] Berman, E. G. and others. (1999). "The Limitations of Regional Peacekeeping."

Therefore to minimize risk and safeguard the lives of its forces, in 1956 the UN amended the principle of non-use of force to allow resort to use of light arms in self-defence only.[48]This new principle was first applied when the United Nations Emergency Force (UNEF I) was deployed in the Suez Canal crisis in November 1956. With regard to this new addition to doctrine, the then UN Secretary-General, Dag Hammarskjold, asserted that

> "...where the rule is applied men engaged in the operation may never take the initiative in the use of armed force, but are entitled to respond with force to an attack with arms, including attempts to make them withdraw from positions which they occupy under orders from the commander, acting under the authority of the Assembly and within the scope of its resolutions."[49]

Peacekeeping and International Relations Vol. 28 (4), p. 2.

[48] *UN General Assembly Document A/3943.* United Nations, New York, Par. 178.
[49] *UN General Assembly Document A/3943.* United Nations, New York, Par. 178.

From then, until the end of the cold-war era in 1988, the UN has continued to apply the principle of use of force for the purpose of self-defence only.

The use of force by the UN has caused debate ever since the organization's earliest days. Some argue that the use of force is unnecessary and irrelevant. They justify this by saying that the use of force means violating the principle of consent by questioning the impartial position of the UN force. Rather than risk clashes between the UN force and the party/ parties, the UN should look for peaceful ways of resolving differences, as preferable and more appropriate than seeking military solution. Such authorities advocate the non-use of force as more consistent with the consent reached with all parties to the UN involvement. "Differences between peacekeepers and the parties involved should be resolved amicably and the use of force would be both unnecessary and counterproductive, in the sense that the use of force against a particular party would abrogate the principle of impartiality." [50]

Others argue for the use of a significant degree of force beyond self-defence to maintain law and order wherever necessary. UN forces need to be flexible to handle changing conflict issues and environments. Sometimes the performance of the original mandate has led to additional tasks that did not accord with the "golden" principles and practices of peacekeeping which have been outlined above.[51] One example of this is the UN mission in the Congo, United Nations Operation in the Congo (ONUC) in February 1961. Initially, it was established to ensure the withdrawal of Belgian forces, to assist the government in maintaining law and order and to provide technical assistance.

> Following the murder of Congolese prime minister Lumumba, the function

---

[50] Lui, F.T. (1992). "United Nations Peacekeeping and the Non-use of Force." *International Peace Academy Occasional Paper Series.* Boulder, Lynne Rienner, pp. 11-12.
[51] Malan. "A Concise History of UN Peace Operations," pp. 20-21.

of ONUC was subsequently modified to include more use of coercive measures to maintain the territorial integrity and political independence of the Congo, preventing the occurrence of civil war and securing the removal from the Congo of all foreign military and mercenaries prompting the breakaway of the country.[52]

The UN faced military attacks while fulfilling its mission in Congo and could only manage to maintain peace and order in Congo by using more coercive measures. However, in post-Cold War intervention, there is a consensus among academics, policy analysts, and politicians that the traditional peacekeeping operations should be still the model wherever this is applicable. For example, in its post-Cold War interventions like those in Namibia, El Salvador, Cambodia, Mozambique, the Gulf, and Haiti, the UN gained successes by applying its traditional principles of monitoring the peaceful settlement agreed by the actors in the conflict.[53] In

---

[52] Bailey and Daws. *The Procedure of the Security Council*, pp. 486-487.
[53] Mohamed, S. (1996). "Managing Conflict After the Cold War." *Peace Review* Vol. 8 (4), p. 9.

others, as in Somalia, it undertook coercive measures, with less happy results, as this study will show. However, the study will focus in the first instance, on the patterns of intervention during the Cold War and the role superpowers played in international peacekeeping missions. The ideological competition and rivalry between superpowers blocked constructive developments of peacekeeping operations during the Cold War years. The Security Council was forced to confine any peacekeeping mission to circumstances in which the peacekeeping agenda conformed to the national interest of the two superpowers, or at least where they were both prepared to consent. Despite its mandate of maintaining international peace and security, which is set out in the first article of the UN Charter, the superpowers' competition for global influence and geo-strategic interest denied the Security Council the power to operate at fuller capacity irrespective of how serious the threat to the peace might be. In line with this, Gumbi Leslie has noted that

> The UN charter had envisaged unanimous purpose prevailing in the

event of having to keep and even enforce peace. Instead, the use of the right to veto by the permanent members of the Security Council blocked many efforts to use the Security Council as an effective instrument for peacekeeping.[54]

For instance, right throughout the Cold War, the Soviet Union was unwilling to contribute to the cost of the vast majority of the UN operations not considered to be in Soviet interests.[55] The Soviets and Americans had differences with regard to the power vested in the Secretary-General and the role of his office in international peacekeeping. The Americans supported the idea of strengthening the Secretary-General while the Soviets advocated empowering the Security Council.[56]

---

[54] Gumbi, L. (1995). "Peacekeeping: Historical Background" in Cilliers, J. and Mills, G. (eds.) *Peacekeeping in Africa.* Johannesburg, Institute for Security Studies and South African Institute of International Affairs Vol. 2, p. 24.
[55] Campbell and others. "Superpowers and UN Peacekeeping," p. 24.
[56] Campbell and others. "Superpowers and UN Peacekeeping," p. 24.

These differences reflected differences of philosophy of international organizations and the balance of power in the UN at that time. Throughout the history of the UN, the location of responsibility for peace and security has been a contested issue among the Security Council, General Assembly, Secretary-General, and regional bodies. Factors like the need to recognize "power realities" as well as the imperatives of efficient delivery and democratic accountability have been involved. These factors have always had to be seen in the context of political rivalries in international relations as well as on their own merits.

While these issues continue to affect UN peacekeeping, a new problem has arisen with the end of the Cold War. The UN charter does not make explicit provision for "failed states" like Somalia,[57] and the range of participating actors and interests is

---

[57] Kittani, I. (1994). "UN Peace Efforts in Somalia." Clements, K. and Wilson, C. (eds.) *UN at the Crossroads*. Peace Research Centre, Australian National University, Canberra, p. 135.

much wider than the original framers of the charter could have envisaged. Any contemporary international peacekeeping mission involves a wide range of sometimes competing interests as well as diverse approaches to the principles and practice of intervention. Among these new approaches is the strategy of cultivating stronger working relationships with regional bodies to tackle security problems within their respective areas of influence.

Chapter Seven: The UN, Regional Bodies, and Peacekeeping

The UN Charter, at Article 52, endorsed the delegation of responsibility to regional arrangements or agencies to handle their respective regional security problems. They were empowered to seek peaceful solutions, provided that these arrangements or agencies and their activities are consistent with the purposes and principles of the United Nations. Furthermore, the UN charter empowers these appropriate regional bodies to take enforcement measures if necessary. With regard to this point, article 53 states that where appropriate, the Security Council shall utilize such regional arrangements or agencies for enforcement action. But no enforcement action is to be taken under regional arrangements or by regional agencies without the authorization of the Security Council. This principle is not always adhered to. For example, the case of Southern African Development Community's (SADC) intervention in the DRC and Lesotho (which this study will discuss) was not authorized by the UN.

Despite its acknowledgment of the existence and roles to be played by these regional arrangements and agencies, the UN charter does not define what these bodies are. Since the 1960s, international relations scholars have discussed the problem of defining regions and regional sub-systems. This study takes Alagappa Muthiah's definition as a working model. He defined "regional arrangements" as cooperation among governments or non-governmental organizations in three or more geographically proximate and interdependent countries for the pursuit of mutual gain in one or more issue-areas.[58] In addition, "regional agencies" refers to formal and informal regional organizations (with physical and organizational infrastructure, staff, budget, etc.) with

---

[58] Muthiah, A. (1997). "Regional Institutions, the UN and International Security: A Framework for Analysis." *Third World Quarterly* Vol. 18 (3), p. 424.

responsibility for implementing regional arrangements.[59]

The case for using regional organizations in peace and security issues rests on the following arguments.

- Those states who comprise regional organizations often understand regional circumstances best or have local knowledge and, in most cases, a common language, have a higher interest in ensuring regional peace and stability than others, and are more readily granted legitimacy as peacekeepers.

- It is believed that regional actors may be better placed than the UN to exert diplomatic [60]pressure using prominent regional personalities.

- Regional involvement in conflict resolution can both lighten the burden of the Security Council and contribute to a deeper sense of participation,

---

[59] Muthiah. "Regional Institutions," p. 424.
[60] Campbell and others. "Superpowers and UN Peacekeeping," pp. 28-29.

consensus and democratization in international affairs. [61]

The recent UN failure in Somalia, Rwanda, and Bosnia made the UN look to regional bodies to address the growing gap between demand and supply, which has arisen from the UN's political, financial, personnel, and operational inadequacies in the face of conflicts arising from collapsing states.[62] Former UN Secretary-General Boutros-Boutros Ghali, also highlighted this fact in his words, "regional arrangements or agencies in many cases possess a potential that should be utilized."[63]

Besides the UN's inadequacies, other factors help make the case for regional contribution to peacekeeping.

The growing desire of regional powers and respective regional or sub-regional organizations to take care of their security problems, to seek greater

---

[61] Muthiah. "Regional Institutions," p. 421.
[62] Muthiah. "Regional Institutions," p. 422.
[63] Muthiah. "Regional Institutions," p. 422.

control over their strategic environment, and growth of economic regionalism are among the factors promoting regionalization of international politics.[64] Since the end of the Cold War, some regional and sub-regional bodies have extended their responsibilities to include a new mandate to address security problems within their respective geographical boundaries. This is because they are the immediate recipients of "collateral damage" from conflicts within the region.

Despite these positive indications, there are limitations to the potential of regional peacekeeping operations.

- The positive strength of "local knowledge" (of regional organizations) is balanced by weakness in their lack of impartiality. They are regularly accused by parties to a local conflict of representing the national prejudices of their most powerful member(s). Consequently, combatants in the region might prefer a peacekeeper from a

---

[64] Muthiah. "Regional Institutions," p. 422.

distant part of the world, rather than from of the neighborhood itself.[65]

- Regional operations can be weakened by lack of mandate and organizational shortcomings[66] (for example, the limbo over the functioning of SADC's security organ.

- Internal conflict can hamper the work of regional organizations. For instance, members of the Inter Governmental Authority on Development (IGAD) involve themselves intra-regional conflicts (like the Sudanese and Somalian civil wars), and tit-for-tat games of retaliation among its member states (Ethiopia and Sudan) and armed border conflict (Ethiopia and Eritrea).

- West African peacekeeping force, the Economic Community of West African States Cease-fire Monitoring Group (ECOMOG) suffers from

---

[65] Chipman, J. (1995). "What Do We Understand by Peacekeeping Today?" Cilliers and Mills (eds.). *Peacekeeping in Africa,* p. 15.
[66] Muthiah. "Regional Institutions," p. 422.

limited resources and logistics while conducting interventions in Liberia and Sierra Leone.

Bearing these problems in mind, regional and sub-regional organizations need to transform themselves to operate within the framework of the UN for successful articulation to take place between the two levels of peacekeeping. How such partnerships between the UN and regional bodies might be achieved, will be discussed in the following section.

Chapter Eight: Ways to Establish Good Working Relationships Between the UN and Regional Bodies

First of all, to build effective task and burden-sharing relationships between the UN and regional institutions requires an understanding of the possibilities and limitations of each as well as the development of principles, rules, and procedures to govern such a partnership.[67] The fact is that marriage between the UN and regional agencies cannot be easily achieved and certainly not by some "quick-fix."

Policy debate is required, as well as critical evaluation and assessment of the roles, tasks, and commitments that are allowed or prohibited by the legal principles and purposes of the charter or constitution of these institutions. It is not enough to evaluate the "paper provisions." It is also necessary to see whether practice has deviated from them[68] and

---

[67] Muthiah. "Regional Institutions," p. 423.
[68] Muthiah. "Regional Institutions," p. 423.

to help either to weed out obstacles within the modus operandi of these institutions or modify their principles and moral obligations to meet the demands of the UN requirements. It also needs political will and approval of the member states of the regional institution to welcome any attempt at restructuring. This, after all, may cause partial or complete shift from the organization's primary objectives in which members may feel they have a historical investment. This task of building institutional capacity is a lengthy process, but the need is for speedy interventions. Skilled expertise drawn both from the UN and regional actors including administrators, military, and civilian personnel (senior diplomats, peace-brokers, mediators, and negotiators) are required. Funds in communication networks to establish direct command and control are also required. However, regional organizations need more than these specific requirements. In fact, they need overall structural transformation. However, to adapt regional organizations to conform to the UN principles is not an easy task. This is because:

- Regional institutions differ so much in terms of purpose, structure, and capacity[69] from the UN that it is difficult to dovetail the missions of global and regional institutions. As Muthiah has observed, regional institutions like the Organization of African Unity (OAU) have been established to favour the ruling incumbents to stay in power against domestic opposition and democratic demands for "good-governance." [70] The OAU's partial stand in member states' internal conflicts, and especially its reluctance to become involved in domestic conflicts at all, have inevitably made it the target of much criticism within and outside Africa. With regard to this, former Tanzanian president Julius Nyerere once said, "The OAU exists only for the protection of the African Heads of State"[71]

---

[69] Muthiah. "Regional Institutions," p. 423.
[70] Muthiah. "Regional Institutions," p. 431.
[71] Yassin El-Ayoutty. (1994). 'OAU for the Future' in El-Ayoutty (ed.). *The Organization of African Unity Thirty Years On.* Westport, Co: Greenwood, p. 179.

President Isayas Afeworki of Eritrea has also accused the OAU of not involving itself in Eritrea's struggle, Africa's longest war for independence.[72] It is too early to say yet whether the various schemes that were put forward for Africa's regeneration in 2001 and the reworking of the OAU into the African Union will affect this situation for the better. Along the same lines as the OAU, the primary rationale for the Gulf Cooperation Council (GCC) is the protection of incumbent monarchs and their conservative kingdoms.[73] To transform these regional bodies from satisfying the interests of the founders themselves, and to substitute its commitment to the wellbeing of the entire region, would mean substantial political risks for the existing rulers of member states. Making their regional bodies conform to the UN modus operandi, may challenge their internal power structures.

---

[72] *Africa Report.* (1993). Vol. 38 (5), p. 6.
[73] *The Gulf Cooperation Council: Record and Analysis.* (1998) Charlottesville, NC: University of North Carolina Press, pp. 1-11.

- It is difficult for the UN to select the most appropriate regional institution to establish partnership because several regional and sub-regional organizations might exist with overlapping responsibilities within the region.[74] For example, in Africa, some strongly believe that OAU should take the responsibility to deal with conflict issues while others would put the burden onto sub-regional bodies. Unless this difference is reconciled at continental level, the UN will have problems in citing its co-operation with Africans to conduct peacekeeping operations. In order to avoid these problems, member states should clearly define and specify the duties and mandate of all regional bodies, based on their relevance to political, economic, security or social issues. The UN has a potential role to play this. For example, it can help devise structural and constitutional frameworks, or in drafting constitutions with regard to new tasks in the area of conflict resolution and management.

---

[74] Muthiah. "Regional Institutions," p. 423.

Relatively speaking, the UN has the appropriate mandate, legitimacy, structure, and greater access to resources. Also, it is often the most impartial and preferred means for extra-regional involvement in local conflicts.[75] Once an appropriate regional security organization is selected, the UN should establish partnership with it, based on its charter (arts. 52 and 53), granting regional bodies the necessary financial, transport, and logistical support and deploying its forces wherever the impartiality of regional peacekeepers is under suspicion or at a minimum, to monitor the impartiality of the already on-duty regional forces.

However, as Campbell and his colleagues have confirmed the view that working out arrangements to govern the contribution of UN peacekeeping with regional peacemaking will pose a difficult challenge.[76] The governing regulations and

---

[75] Muthiah. "Regional Institutions," pp. 422-23.
[76] Campbell and others. "Superpowers and the UN Peacekeeping," p. 29.

understandings of peacekeeping, which shape regional bodies' policies towards conflict resolution, can pose major problems for relations with UN peacekeeping. For example, as we have seen, the OAU's founding and long-standing principles of sovereignty and non-intervention in the internal affairs of its member countries stand in a way of effective peacekeeping. There is as of yet no indication that its successor, the AU will take up the problem with determination. In the former Yugoslavia, NATO exceeded the political-legal authority granted to it by the UN. Not only did it act beyond the control and approval of the UN but it also questioned the UN's principle of consent and impartiality.[77] The UN Secretary-General reported that, while the undertaking of parallel operations by ECOWAS and the UN in Liberia broke fresh ground in peacekeeping, finding a joint concept of operation

---

[77] Chipman. "What Do We Understand by Peacekeeping?", pp. 15-16.

was not easy.[78] Lack of uniformity and problems of politico-military command and control between the UN and regional forces make the problems worse in the following ways:

- The level of skill and training at regional level is not up to the standard of the UN missions. [79]

- The lack of communication in circulating information between the UN and regional bodies, which is mostly due to the absence of intelligence reports on the dynamics of current conflict situations.[80]

- Regional organizations are in most cases suffering from lack of funds to perform their regional peacekeeping mandates.[81]

---

[78] *Eleventh Progress Report of the Secretary-General of the United Nations Observer Missions in Liberia, S/1995/473.* (1995). United Nations, New York.

[79] Berman and others. "The Limitations of Regional Peacekeeping," p. 2.

[80] Berman and others. "The Limitations of Regional Peacekeeping," p. 2.

[81] Berman and others. "The Limitations of Regional Peacekeeping," p. 2.

In additions to attempts to transform regional bodies, the UN itself also needs to be strengthened to play a leading role to maintain international peace and order.

Chapter Nine: Empowering the UN to Play a Leading Role in Maintaining International Peace and Security

Not only do the regional organizations need peacekeeping capacity-building, but the UN itself needs upgrading and transformation. The fact is that the UN structure came into existence based on post-WWII realities. The original assumptions cannot be responsive to the changes in the global security environment which have taken place in the five decades since then. It is also worth noting that the original Charter was signed by fewer than a quarter of the present member states. At present, the composition of the Security Council reflects the world as it was in 1945, with the victors of the Second World War exercising an overriding influence over questions relating to international peace and security.[82] However, efforts have been

---

[82] Field, S. and Murphy, C. N. (1998). "United Nations Reform: Perspectives from the South and the North." Johannesburg. *Foundation for Global Dialogue Occasional Paper No. 14,* p. 13.

under way to address the UN's shortcomings to manage international security problems, among them:

- The idea of democratizing the UN, by establishing equal representation and a general restructuring program. These ideas were proposed by the Open-Ended Working Group on the Question of Equitable Representation on and Increase in Membership of the Security Council, which was held in May 1997 under the office of the president of the General Assembly and two vice Chairmen. After having informal consultation with 165 member countries, as of 1993, they proposed expansion in both the permanent and non-permanent membership, which would increase the size of the Security Council to 26. It was proposed that in the permanent category, five seats could be added from Africa, Asia, Latin America, and two industrialized states. An additional five seats could also be added in the non-permanent category and distributed among Asia, Latin America, Eastern Europe, and two African states.[83] It has been argued that the more representative the Security Council the more legitimate its actions will seem and the easier it will be to build consensus and have its action carried out.[84] Permanent members of the Security Council, like the United States, France, Britain, and Russia are opposed to the enlargement of the Security Council,[85] claiming that too many members will hamstring the Council and paralyze decision-making. They fear that the larger the Council, the more their influence will be diluted.[86] Moreover, the permanent members of the Security Council are blamed for using

---

[83] Field and Murphy. "United Nations Reform," p. 16.

[84] Field and Murphy. "United Nations Reform," p. 13.

[85] Ambassador Bilhari Kausikan. "Do the Permanent Members Really Want Reform."

[86] Field and Murphy. "United Nations Reform," p. 16.

the power invested in them to satisfy their own vital interests. As Paul James observes, the five permanent members have used the Council increasingly as a cover for unilateral action, by seeking tacit agreement for intervention in their sphere of influence.[87]

- It has to be noted that reforming the UN Security Council is not the only factor to be addressed to bring about effective peacekeeping. For example, the UN should undertake a campaign program through its regional offices at different part of the world to establish close working relationships or partnerships with governmental and non-governmental bodies like civil society groups to gain their support. With regard to this, the member countries should offer their citizens opportunities of knowing the UN charter and international law to help the grass roots

---

[87] Paul, J. (1995). "Security Council Reform: Arguments About the Future of the UN System," p. 9. (Cited in Field and Murphy. "United Nations Reform," p. 12).

understand the purpose of the UN missions and to respect its global mandate. In some cases, for example, the UN peacekeeping force has been seen as the US on a mission to satisfy America's interests.[88]

- In August 2000, the office of the UN Secretary-General introduced its so-called the Brahimi report, named after the Algerian former Minister of Foreign Affairs, who led the project.[89] It launched a number of recommendations on how to enhance the capacity of the UN in planning and executing effective international peacekeeping operations. The report seeks ways to strengthen and transform the UN Department of Peacekeeping (DPKO), and the UN Secretariat Department of Political Affairs

---

[88] Dandeker, C. and others. (1997). "The Future of Peace Support Operations: Strategic Peacekeeping and Success." *Armed Forces and Society* Vol. 23 (3), p. 21.

[89] Official Release of the Norwegian Ministry of Foreign Affairs. http://odin.dep.no/ud/engelsh/.

(DPA) to help address all conflict problems in the world today. The report suggests that the UN needs to focus on addressing the roots of conflicts, peace-building strategies, and enhancing contributions of civilian specialists.[90] To perform such tasks the report recommended, [91] the establishment of an Integrated Missions Task Force (IMTF) to help quickly gather expertise from the UN Department of Peacekeeping and the UN system for rapid deployment are needed. Other functions of this body would be the improvement of the UN information network, fund raising to sustain lengthy peace-building processes and increasing the political willingness and commitment of troop contributing countries for peacekeeping missions of longer duration.

---

[90] Official Release of the Norwegian Ministry of Foreign Affairs. http://odin.dep.no/ud/engelsh/.
[91] Official Release of the Norwegian Ministry of Foreign Affairs

The UN can also succeed in its peace support operations by dispatching information with regard to its objectives to the warring parties, not only before involvement but also during the course of the intervention. The warring parties on their side also need to abide by their agreement to welcome the peacekeepers during the entire course of the peacekeeping operation. Moreover, The UN should maintain its primary responsibility for international peace and convince or even force other regional bodies to revise their constitutions in case of conflict with the UN peacekeeping mandate. Of special importance is the understanding in article 52 (1) and 53, to work under UN leadership. As the only legitimate body to undertake intervention, the UN should mobilize member states to take part in peacekeeping missions, without calculating their national interests, in response to the call from the international organization to settle ongoing intra or interstate conflicts that have global security implications. This demands that irrespective of their economic and military strength, every member country should be willing to participate under the authority of the UN. Unilateral involvement of any peacekeeping effort is fraught with destabilizing potential, for example, the US debacle in its intervention in Somalia.[92]

These are ambitious and far-reaching requirements, which echo the ambiguities and contradictions noted earlier in the case of the League. The necessary requirements include states having to develop common values around common security issues irrespective of considering their vital interests at stake. Collective security would only work with all members fully dedicated to the achievements of national interest within the context of maintaining international peace and order. These would also help the UN to prepare itself to deal with the complex nature of conflict in the post-Cold War world.

---

[92] Landsberg, C. (1996). "Pretoria's Catch-22 Dilemma." *West Africa,* p. 1670.

Chapter Ten: Peacekeeping in the Post-Cold War World: Reason for New Approach

Freedman notes that some of the most symptomatic changes of the post-Cold War world altered the nature and status of intervention.[93] The most significant global event that altered the nature of intervention was the rapid decay of the socialist system under the leadership of the former Soviet Union and its collapse towards the end of 1980s. The disappearance of the Soviet Union as a principal actor in the global system had direct political ramifications on the politics of the Third World in the aftermath of the Cold War and also produced major changes in the context of intervention. Some observers noted that the Third World internal conflicts which were suppressed by either or both of the two antagonist superpowers now found outlets to express themselves openly and demanded

---

[93] Sharp, J. M. O. (1994). "Appeasement, Intervention and the Future of Europe." Freedman, L. (ed.). *Military Intervention in European Conflicts.* Oxford, Blackwell, pp. 34-55.

international intervention.[94] This also means that, as Barry Buzan notes, this loss of ideological motive and pullback of the superpowers after the cold-war era had two potentially contradictory effects on military security in the Third World.

In the first place, it meant cuts in the level of the military, financial, and ideological support available from the center to support conflicts in the periphery. In Africa, dictators who had been propped up by superpower aid and military hardware were left without the means by which to maintain power.[95] Examples include the regimes of Said Barre of Somalia, Mengistu Haile Mariam of Ethiopia, and Samuel Doe of Liberia, all of which collapsed in 1991 due to withdrawal of external military assistance. The overthrow of these dictators threatened anarchy in numerous cases, forcing the

---

[94] Johnston, A. (1995). *Democratizing Intervention? Intervention and the Foreign Policy Debate in Post-Apartheid South Africa.* Paper delivered to a Conference of the European Consortium on Political Research (ECPR), Paris, p. 2.
[95] Field and Murphy. "United Nations Reform." p. 14.

Security Council to become involved as the primary organ to take care of international peace and security.[96]

Secondly, it meant more freedom for local security dynamics to operate without the constraint of outside interest and intervention.[97] In addition to Buzan's arguments, one can also argue that the western call for democratization caused adverse impacts by reviving ethnic and minority questions within the Third World authoritarian single party rule. The study will discuss this issue in more detail in the next section within an African context. Inter-state war is also evident in former colonial territories due to the arbitrary boundaries drawn by the colonial powers. This study will also emphasize this issue in the following section.

---

[96] Field and Murphy. "United Nations Reform," p. 15.
[97] Buzan, B. (1994). "National Security in the Post-Cold War Third World." *Strategic Review for Southern Africa.* Midrand, Institute for Strategic Studies Vol. 16 (1), p. 8.

During the Cold War, many states in the Third World enjoyed only "external sovereignty," supported by the UN and other continental and regional organizations. This principle of "all states are sovereign equals," rather than internal legitimacy and recognition as the true basis of sovereignty, led Robert Jackson, in an influential analysis, to refer to these Third World states as "quasi-states."[98] This means that their sovereignty is largely constructed externally by other states recognizing them as legal equals. They are accorded diplomatic rights, a seat in the UN, regional bodies, the right to their own flags, and their representatives at international forums and embassies in foreign countries. This external recognition has not been dependent on internal reality, that is on whether the state commanded internal sovereignty in the sense of effective administration and military control over its territory,

---

[98] Jackson, R. H. (1990). *Quasi-States: Sovereignty, International Relations and the Third World.* Cambridge, Cambridge University Press, Chapter 1.

as well as the power of taxation and legitimacy among the ruled.[99] The fact is that some of these states lacked internal legitimacy and cohesiveness and had little chance of internal resources to govern effectively.[100] The superpowers gave aid (both military and financial) to keep authoritarian regimes in power. In doing so, they played down or even ignored the recipients' poor human right records and undemocratic rule. For instance, by the 1970s, the three largest recipients of American development assistance in Africa were the regimes of pro-West dictators, Mobutu Sese Seko in Zaire, Sergeant Samuel Doe in Liberia, and General Said Barre of Somalia.[101] The USSR contributed to this situation by giving aid to Mengistu Haile Mariam in Ethiopia. In 1994, John Mueller argued that "at one time the

---

[99] Buzan. "National Security in the Post-Cold War," pp. 13-14.
[100] Buzan. "National Security in the Post-Cold War" pp. 13-14.
[101] Stremlau, J. and others. (2000). *Putting People First: Priorities for Africa and the Millennium Assembly.* Johannesburg, South African Institute of International Affairs, p. 4.

United States had to treat Mobutu of Zaire as a dictator who had brought his country to ruin but who was on the right side in the Cold War. After the Cold War, it could—indeed had to—treat him merely as a dictator who has brought his country to ruin."[102] Coincidentally, the demise of the Cold War made the East and West find themselves on the same side of many conflicts.[103] The Soviets, in particular, undertook a radical change of direction in foreign policy under its "new" thinking. This was targeted towards the universal acceptability of peacekeeping "…an improved international climate and future prospects of peacekeeping as a technique in international conflict management motivated by international political, economic and security implications." [104]

---

[102] John, M. (1994). "The Catastrophe Quota: Trouble After the Cold War." *Journal of Conflict Resolution*. Vol. 38 (3), p. 25.
[103] John. "The Catastrophe Quota," p. 29.
[104] Campbell and others. "Superpowers and United Nations Peacekeeping," p. 24.

In short, the aftermath of the Cold War witnessed the end of aid to regimes which were now disposable (but not to others like Egypt, and Israel which were still strategically and politically important) and the former superpowers tried to force their clients to solve their internal problems in peaceful ways. The Soviets came to understand the internal conflicts in the Third World as increasingly explicable by ethnicity, clan, and religious factors rather than to the influence of imperialism.[105] Certainly it became convenient for them to do so. These trends were accompanied by a reduction in the level of Soviet enthusiasm for revolutionary insurgency in most of the Third World and preference for political rather than military settlement of these insurgent conflicts.[106] For example, Soviet commentators replaced their qualified enthusiasm for insurgent struggle notably in Southern Africa with an

---

[105] Campbell and others. "Superpowers and United Nations Peacekeeping," p. 24.
[106] Macfarlane, N. S. (1990). "Superpower Rivalry in the 1990s." *Third World Quarterly* Vol. 12 (1), p. 11.

endorsement of negotiation leading to an orderly and peaceful transition to majority rule.[107] In the economic sphere as well, the Soviets exhorted their Third World clients to improve their economic performance and reduce the burden they imposed on the Soviet economy. The chosen means were through internal reforms to expand the sphere of opportunity open to private initiatives and through the expansion of trading and investment ties to the developed Western economies.[108] The prescriptions were indistinguishable from those of western states themselves.

The Soviet economy had in any case deteriorated dramatically towards the close of 1970s, making the burden of activism in the Third World harder to bear, and diverting the attention of policymakers to internal issues and to the development of foreign

---

[107] The embrace of armed insurgency in Central America characteristic of the early 1980s has largely disappeared. Likewise, enthusiasm for insurgent struggle as a means of resolving the South African question has dampened.

[108] Macfarlane. "Superpower Rivalry in the 1990s," p. 12.

polices which could permit them to address their domestic problems more effectively. Most prominent among such policies were a reduction of tensions with the West and especially the US. In turn, the Soviet Union would gain from a reduction of the pressure of military competition, (security) as well as enhanced access to western technologies and expertise useful for coping with the problems of economic restructuring.[109]

It is possible to say that the new Soviet policy shift opened bigger opportunities for the UN to work out its mandate as a guardian of international peace and security. The Soviet's new thinking on international conflict management which resulted in the de-ideologization of peacekeeping[110] had the potential to improve dramatically the environment in which the UN operated. In 1989, superpower mediation,

---

[109] A report on a conference of African Marxists in Accra not surprisingly concluded that the South could not depend on the USSR for meaningful assistance for transition to socialism.
[110] Macfarlane. "Superpower Rivalry in 1990s," p. 15.

exemplified in Africa, (Angola, Namibia, Ethiopia), Southeast Asia (Afghanistan and Cambodia), and Latin America (Nicaragua), indicated that the superpowers' veto squabbles in the UN Security Council were at an end. Interest in the potential role of the UN as a mediator and executor of political settlements correspondingly rose.[111] For instance, changing Soviet perspectives on the UN were evident in the Soviet decision to pay its back dues on peacekeeping operations and in support of the UN's supervisory role in Namibia's transition to independence under resolution 435.[112] The Soviet Union had further proved its commitment to its new foreign policy by withdrawing its military forces from Afghanistan.[113] At the beginning of November 1989, the US and the Soviet Union jointly sponsored

---

[111] Campbell and others. "Superpowers and United Nations Peacekeeping," p. 28.

[112] Macfarlane. "Superpower Rivalry in the 1990s," p. 13.

[113] The USSR originally opposed resolution 435 as a basis for Namibian Settlement. Cited in Macfarlane. "Superpowers Rivalry in the 1990s," p. 13.

a General Assembly resolution and gave a press conference—both firsts at the UN—calling for the organization to play a greater role in maintaining peace and fostering international cooperation.[114] As of 1989, the Soviet Union joined the US in providing the initial transportation of contingents to operational areas free of charge to the UN.[115]

Despite the end of the Cold War in 1989, which resulted in the former superpowers' coming together over peacekeeping, a lasting solution to the fresh kind of intra-state conflict and total state collapse evidenced in some of the Third World countries after the end of the Cold War in the 1990s could not necessarily be expected. As Johnston has observed, unlike the conflicts during the Cold War, most of the conflicts in the aftermath of the Cold War world have involved state collapse, induced by ethnic strife, secession, or "inchoate civil upheaval" rather than

---

[114] Campbell and others. "Superpowers and United Nations Peacekeeping," p. 24.
[115] Campbell and others. "Superpower and United Nations Peacekeeping," p. 25.

the inter-state conflict.[116] However, at least the superpower dominance over the UN veto system to satisfy their own ideological interest and expand their sphere of influence exists no more. Still, the dominance of US and the less certain influence of regional powers like South Africa is very real. Otherwise, it is possible to argue that the way is open for more chances to conduct intervention involving multinational peacekeepers within and outside of the UN structure, such as involving regional and sub-regional organizations.

In several cases, the cutting of external assistance paved the way for internal insurgencies to take advantage and overthrow the old regimes. For instance, in the early 1990s, the ruling regimes of Zaire, Ethiopia, Somalia, and Liberian were deposed.[117] Abandonment by external supporters and the intensification of domestic military challenge played their part in state failure in these cases. Failed states occur where the state apparatus decays and is

---

[116] Johnston. *Democratizing Intervention,* p. 2.
[117] Stremlau and others. *Putting People First*, p. 4.

unable to exercise physical control and sovereignty within its formally defined territories. Government power of taxation, and administrative power of rural and distant urban areas are eroded to the point of collapse.[118] In such circumstances, ruling regimes are replaced by oppositions which are hardly better (as in Zaire, Liberia, and Ethiopia) or are doomed to a ceaseless civil war like Somalia.

The dramatic change in the nature of conflict, most of which was now intra-state, made it difficult to apply the restricted principles of UN intervention after the end of Cold War. Consent, non-use, or minimum use of force and impartiality were difficult to apply in the new circumstances no matter how well they had served in the past. Intervention can now be mounted without the consent of the warring parties, undertaking more coercive measures than during the Cold War intervention.

---

[118] Herbst, J. (1997). "Africa's Failed States." *South African Yearbook of International Affairs*. Johannesburg, South African Institute of International Affairs, p. 334.

In the 1990s, military operations in support of peacekeeping increased in number, size, scope, task, and complexity.[119] For instance, from 1988-98, thirty-six new peacekeeping operations were undertaken in comparison to fifteen in the forty years of Cold War peacekeeping operations.[120] These missions employed more than 80,000 personnel as against only 10,000 before 1987. Seventy-seven countries provided these troops at a cost of over US 3.5 billion dollars in interventions between 1990-1994, while before 1990 the figure was only 400 million.[121] These figures exclude the cost of other operations like those undertaken by the US in Somalia and ECOWAS in Liberia referring to UN operations alone.

---

[119] Dandeker and others. "The Future of Peace Support Operations," p. 21.
[120] Mills and Cilliers. *From Peacekeeping to Managing Complex Emergencies,* p. 1.
[121] Mills, G. (1996). "South Africa and Peacekeeping." *South African Yearbook of International Affairs.* Johannesburg, South African Institute of International Affairs, p. 214.

In this respect, the number of role players in peacekeeping efforts has significantly increased. Regional bodies including the OAU, NATO and ECOWAS have become prominent. Western powers indulge in peacekeeping on their own account. The US intervention in Somalia, Haiti, and France in Burundi provide examples of this.

In terms of scope, peacekeeping missions have involved new ingredients like humanitarian intervention and building political conditions for sustainable democratic systems as a lasting solution or at the least, post-conflict peace building. The latter is emphasized by the former UN Secretary-General Boutros-Boutros-Ghali. According to him, "Post-Conflict Peace Building" is a critical link in the cycle of UN peace actions:

> Preventive diplomacy seeks to resolve disputes before violence breaks out: peacemaking and keeping are required to halt conflicts and preserve peace once it is obtained. If successful, they strengthen the opportunity for post-conflict peace building, which can prevent the recurrence

of violence among nations and
peoples [122]

These involve developing and/or implementing a
political transition after an end to military hostilities
and the reform or establishment of basic state
institutions like police and judicial systems.
Supervising and monitoring democratic elections
towards the formation of new governments also
come under the heading.[123]

With respect to this function, the UN did manage to
achieve success in some of its nation-building
missions. Nicaragua (1989-92), El Salvador (1991-
1995), Cambodia (1989-1990), Mozambique (1992-
1995), and Namibia (1989-1990) are examples. In
other places like Sierra Leone, Somalia, Angola,
Liberia, Haiti, Rwanda, and the Western Sahara, the

---

[122] Boutros-Gali, B. (1992). "Agenda for Peace
Preventive Diplomacy, Peacemaking and
Peacekeeping." Report of the Secretary-General.
[123] Eva, B. (1995). "Reinventing Governments: The
Promise and Perils of United Nations Peace
Building." *Journal of Conflict Resolution* Vol. 39
(3), pp. 388-389.

UN's efforts to settle war-torn societies continue. As the case of Somalia appears to show, the UN's nation-building vision seems hardly possible in societies which have suffered such trauma. Arguably, only nations themselves can make their own state by peace or war. The problem is particularly acute in Africa. From a historical point of view, modern African states were formed by colonizers in their own image rather than grounded on African realities and knowledge. The UN attempts to restore failed states in Africa to their former shape and geographical picture will not bring lasting solution in the sense the process is a repetition of the colonial mistake. Africa may go through more conflict and bloodshed just like 19th century Europe. This study will give more attention to this issue as it develops.

Post-Cold War peacekeeping sanctioned more use of force than during Cold-War interventions. The post-Cold War period has witnessed the emergence of the problem of so-called "failed" states. In response, the UN has taken on a new mandate of greater military involvement with the aim of enforcing the peace where lawlessness has taken over. The UN's old principle of consent, and non-use of military force has become seriously compromised and has lost considerable ground in the profile of 1990s peacekeeping. Interventions have been conducted in situations where conflict has not yet been terminated at the time of international deployment. The concept of peacekeeping has been broadened to encompass new, more "muscular" and forceful forms of operation, which indeed require the use of force.[124] The reason for this has been, as in the case of Somalia, the state apparatus has totally collapsed as the result of vicious civil wars. Under these circumstances it has been difficult to maintain the UN Cold War principle of consent and impartiality which allowed UN and actors in the conflicts to sign the deployment of the UN neutral peacekeeping force. During the Cold War, the UN peacekeepers were tasked to monitor agreements (like cease-fires)

---

[124] Dandeker and others. "The Future of Peace Support Operations," p. 22.

that had already been reached by the conflicting parties.[125] In the post-Cold War pattern of intervention, the UN had intervened in the intra-state conflicts without invitations from the warring parties to contain the disaster of the war on the civilian population. This was despite the fact that the UN in article 2 (7) of the Charter recognized that "nothing contained in the present charter shall authorize the international body to intervene in the matters which are essentially within the domestic jurisdiction of any state," except when the Security Council is agreed to implement enforcement measures under chapter VII. From a moral point of view, many would argue that in case of deadly civil wars like in Somalia, Rwanda, and former Yugoslavia in which war and famine claimed the lives of hundreds of thousands, the UN should not be bound by its principle of non-violability of the sovereignty of states. As Helman and Ramer point out, in the cases of "failed" states, "(the)... traditional view of sovereignty has so

---

[125] Dandeker and others, "The Future of Peace Support Operations," p. 28.

decayed that all should recognize the appropriateness of the UN measures inside member states to save them from self-destruction."[126] The fact that there is no legitimate government within these states, and dozens of factions involved, makes it difficult to secure consent. One can argue that eroding the wall of sovereignty in the absence of a functioning state and central government, as in the case of Somalia, is a necessary thing to do. The only minimum requirement is to give the UN and other humanitarian organizations a chance to deliver humanitarian assistance to the victims.

The idea and practice of developing a greater military dimension under the new peacekeeping model, has faced critical debate and opposition from the advocates of traditional limits to peacekeeping activities. They argue that significant use of force has no place in UN actions because using force means losing consent, an essential requirement for keeping

---

[126] Eva. "Reinventing Governments," p. 392.

peace.[127] Furthermore, they claim the (in context) massive use of force in Somalia by the American and by the UN brought no success but discredited both the UN and the Americans. [128]

These dramatic shifts in the nature of conflicts in the post-Cold War period need a mixture of both traditional and modern peacekeeping approaches. The preceding discussion has shown that classical intervention is not good enough to address the so-called complex emergencies which caused massive civilian crisis and total state collapse. Therefore, a new pattern of intervention needs to be undertaken to handle new causalities and manifestations of conflict. This is forceful humanitarian intervention.

---

[127] Dandeker and others. "The Future of Peace Support Operations," p. 22.
[128] Dandeker and others. "The Future of Peace Support Operations," p. 22.

Chapter Eleven: Changes and Continuities in Patterns of Intervention in the Aftermath of the Cold-War: "Forceful Humanitarian Intervention"

Post-Cold War intervention also involves strategic interest, not least because, with limited resources, some choices have to be made about which crisis should be given priority. [129] The example of the intervention in former Yugoslavia by France and Britain is a case in point.[130] The key objective was to contain the spread and intensity of the conflict. The risk which persistent conflict poses for the economic and social security of the European Union, made it imperative to encourage the conflicting parties to

---

[129] Dandeker and others. "The Future of Peace Support Operations," p. 22.
[130] Dandeker and others. "The Future of Peace Support Operations," p. 22.

reach a settlement, and to mitigate the scale of the humanitarian disaster.[131]

Both "traditional" and "modern" peacekeeping interventions involve coercive and non-coercive means to resolve conflicts based on Chapter VI and VII of the UN Charter. But the difference is in the level of use of force or the application of Chapter VII of the UN Charter. The latter peacekeeping concept involves more use of power. More coercive action should be taken against those who have broken agreements or as a spur to encourage the dispute than in the former peacekeeping model.[132]

In the case of traditional peacekeeping, the parties have decided to settle a dispute and desire to use the UN as an international service in order to assist the peacemaking process. The peacekeepers are following a strategic agenda defined by the parties to the conflict. In the case of contemporary

---

[131] Dandeker and others. "The Future of Peace Support Operations," pp. 24-25.
[132] Dandeker and others. "The Future of Peace Support Operations," pp. 24-25.

peacekeeping, other powers in international society, operating through UN regional arrangements and normally under resolution of the Security Council, take the initiative in providing a force designed to limit the effects of a conflict and assisting in creating the conditions for its termination.[133]

Although post-Cold War intervention depends upon a degree of consent from the conflicting parties, the level of such consent will be given much less weight than in traditional peacekeeping. "Indeed, the legitimacy of the instigation of the mission derives from the authority of the UN and Security Council resolution and less from the consent of the conflicting parties."[134] As some have argued,

> the legal base of post-Cold War peacekeeping action is potentially more fragile than a traditional peacekeeping

---

[133] Dandeker and others. "The Future of Peace Support Operations," p. 25.
[134] Dandeker and others. "The Future of Peace Support Operations," p. 29.

> operation because it is based on a
> less robust environment of
> consent and the initiatives stem
> more from international powers
> than from conflicting parties
> themselves.[135]

But, on the other side of the coin, in cases where the conflicting parties are not willing to welcome the peacekeeping forces, "forceful humanitarian intervention" is a necessary condition without the authorization of the belligerents.

Cold War intervention was mainly conducted to sustain and maintain the existing states and regimes which were allies of the former superpowers while post-Cold War intervention is on humanitarian grounds[136] and in crises of gross violation of human rights within states' jurisdiction. Under this condition, the UN Article 2 (7), which states that the UN is not to intervene in matters which are essentially within the domestic jurisdiction of any state, needs to be revised in order to empower the UN

---

[135] Dandeker and others. "The Future of Peace Support Operations," pp. 29-30.
[136] Dandeker and others. "The Future of Peace Support Operations," pp. 29-30.

to intervene unconditionally to rescue civilians. As a matter of fact, since the Cold War, the UN has been busy addressing internal conflicts. Haití, Cambodia, El Salvador, Georgia, Liberia, Mozambique, Rwanda, Somalia, Sierra Leone, Tajikistan, and DRC are all examples.[137] Despite all these successes, as this study will show, the UN is encountering setbacks while conducting its international peacekeeping missions.

Since post-Cold War peacekeeping involves a number of peacekeepers other than the UN, the problem of command and clashes of interest among stakeholders is inevitable. Each one of the role players has its own principles of peacekeeping and agenda for involvement. This can make the peacekeeping missions far from smooth. For example, regarding the possible tension between the UN and regional bodies, Mohamed Sahnoun has

---

[137] Welch, C. E. "The OAU and Human Rights: Regional Promotion of Human Rights." Yassin El-Ayoutty (ed.). *The Organization of African Unity Thirty Years On*, pp. 53-76.

raised key questions around the confusions of unclear mandates in modern day UN peacekeeping missions, especially in connection with new tasks of the so-called "humanitarian intervention" which were undertaken in Somalia, Bosnia, and Rwanda. Such confusions led in all cases to the withdrawal of the interventionist force. What was expected from this intervention is not clear even now. Did the UN intervene in internal conflicts to make peace between contending parties and preserve or restore national or even regional peace? Or was it to put an end to human rights abuse? Or was it to check humanitarian tragedy? [138]

Reacting to the issues raised by Sahnoun, Robert Jackson argues:

> Because international relations are subjected to diverging and even conflicting normative considerations, what the most responsible choice would be in

---

[138] Dandeker and others. "The Future of Peace Support Operations," p. 30.

any particular case is not something that can be determined in principle [by the UN charter] or in advance. There are no moral philosophies that we can apply to the question of humanitarian intervention in the confident expectation of arriving at a clear judgment one way or the other.[139]

For Sahnoun, Jackson's approach means the UN should be even more politically and psychologically prepared and much better equipped intellectually and technically to deal with the conflicts.

Above all, we must trust people. Go back to the grass roots and trust and strengthen what we might call the natural immunity system. Armed intervention in a humanitarian tragedy should certainly not be ruled out. We should, however, exercise maximum caution and restraint. Let us exhaust all other possibilities before using armed forces.[140]

---

[139] Mohamed. "Managing Conflicts," p. 10.
[140] Mohamed. "Managing Conflicts," p. 10.

In addition, the concept of sovereignty needs to be extended to include the warlords as legitimate political orders who can play a greater role when humanitarian missions in their respective administrative areas are undertaken.

Generally speaking, for the UN to establish effective peacekeeping, it should consider the following possible policy recommendations:

- Minimize the cost of troop reimbursement by recruiting voluntary civilian (doctors, police, and lawyers) and military personnel from member countries. This may help to meet the problem of longer duration and extended tasks of post-conflict state-building, which, in turn, requires the commitment and political will of UN member countries in funding and supplying more personnel than before.[141] The

---

[141] Goulding, M. (1993). "The Evolution of UN Peacekeeping." *International Affairs* Vol. 69 (3), pp. 451-454.

UN also needs to raise fund from donor organizations and NGOs.

- The warring parties should comply with their agreement with the UN. The UN needs to establish good working conditions with local institutions and to help them to build their capacities. Where applicable the UN should still implement its principles, consent, impartiality, and sovereignty.[142] Some also believe that peace building takes the United Nations into a territory unexplored by UN practitioners and uncharted by UN strategists or scholars.[143] Therefore, the UN needs to expand its research capacity and encourage academic institutions and civil society groups to undertake fuller-scale understandings in

---

[142] Goulding. "The Evolution of UN Peacekeeping." p. 451.
[143] Campbell and others "Superpowers and United Nations Peacekeeping" p. 26 Conclusion and Prognosis

the area of conflict management and resolution.

In conclusion, the post-Cold War period has witnessed a greater prevalence of intra-state conflicts than ever before. In response to this shift in the nature of conflict, adaptations of collective security measures have been undertaken to address the incidence of internal state crisis. Dramatic changes in conduct, concept, and approach of peacekeeping have been the result. Among these are forceful humanitarian intervention, more coercive military interventions and post-conflict state building. These have been features of many contemporary peacekeeping missions. Wherever applicable, however, classical peacekeeping approaches and doctrines like consent, impartiality, and minimum use of force have also been used in order to address states internal security problems.

These developments are in line with the most fundamental mandates of the UN. The Preamble of the UN Charter states that the people of the UN are determined

- to save succeeding generations from the scourge of war, which twice in our lifetime has brought untold sorrow to mankind
- to practice tolerance and live together in peace with one another as good neighbors.

Throughout its history, the organization has struggled to give effect to these lofty ideas in a constantly changing political context. Some of its problems arise from its own nature. The UN was formed to create peaceful international relations among states, settle conflicts between them and to undertake collective measures to deter the aggression that leads to global war, but the UN Charter itself has doctrinal constraints. Its Article 2 (7) reads that "Nothing contained in the present Charter shall authorize the United Nations to intervene in matters which are essentially within the domestic jurisdiction of any state or shall require the members to submit such matters to settlement under the Charter; but this principle shall not prejudice the application of enforcement under Chapter VII." This also means that throughout its history, whatever experience and success in resolving conflicts the UN has had, has been with inter-state conflicts rather than intra-state. However, the post-Cold War era has witnessed the emergence of the so-called failed states in the international system. At worst, bloody civil wars have caused the total disappearance of internationally recognised states. For more three decades now, the former Somalia and Yugoslavia have been absent from their seats at the regional and international forums. To respond to the changing nature of conflict, the UN has added new ingredients to classical peacekeeping doctrines. Among these are more use of military means in forceful humanitarian intervention, post-conflict state building to meet the new kind of conflict in what have come to be known as complex emergencies. In the face of these new conditions, the UN is striving to address internal conflicts by making doctrinal shifts. Among these are treating the issue of sovereignty as being more flexible and picking up the rarely-used Article 53 of its Charter (on partnership with regional and sub-regional bodies) to seek for collaborative efforts and common approach in addressing conflicts.

Made in the USA
Columbia, SC
08 December 2023

27484458R00075